THE LITTLE BOOK OF
JESUS

THE LITTLE BOOK OF

JESUS

Priya Hemenway

BARNES
& NOBLE
BOOKS

NEW YORK

This edition published by Barnes & Noble, Inc.,
by arrangement with The Book Laboratory® Inc.

The Little Book of Jesus
©2004 The Book Laboratory® Inc.

Design by Amy Ray
Cover by Amy Ray and Bullet Liongson

2004 Barnes & Noble Books
M 10 9 8 7 6 5 4 3 2 1

ISBN: 0-7607-5447-0

Printed in Singapore

Contents

Introduction 7

The Early Years 11

The Teachings 51

The Final Days 89

The Church 125

Afterword 149

Acknowledgements 150

Introduction

The story of Jesus is a singularly poetic and beautiful one, and twenty centuries have done nothing to diminish it. Set in an ancient land, at a time when little was recorded, the story of Jesus concerns a man whose very life was divine. He came into the world as a Messiah, fulfilling a prophecy that God would deliver the people of Israel from their suffering.

He taught in a gentle way about love and about trust in God. He performed miracles of healing and spoke words of great wisdom. Recognized by some as the Messiah, but disavowed by others, Jesus was eventually crucified for political reasons. He rose, however, into eternal life where he sits on the side of God in a symbolic relationship of supreme blessedness.

The life and teachings of Jesus are based on devotion to God. Speaking out against greed and selfishness, he drew great crowds into his fold. His life was a complex drama in which he cast a wide net and drew close to him men and women of every sort. Jesus gave his life for the truths he believed in and left behind a message of peace. The story was written down for the Christian

Church in various forms in the four Gospels of the New Testament having been passed on as an oral tradition among illiterate people for many years. It has been told endless times in various ways. Although the details of the story are not always consistent, the essence of the message has never been lost. What is written on the following pages is a loosely combined extraction from the Gospel stories. It is not complete, but it conveys the essential message of a most blessed life.

The essence of Jesus' teachings was expressed most eloquently throughout his life, in his actions and his words. He often repeated the two commandments as the fundamentals of his teaching.

The first is this: The Lord our God is one;
you shall love the Lord your God with all your heart,
and with all your soul, and with all your mind, and with all your strength.
The second is this: You shall love your neighbor as yourself.

The Early Years

The details of Jesus' life, as we are most familiar with them, were written down by different men with different sensibilities between forty and one hundred and twenty years after Jesus' death. During those years stories were told and retold thousands of times. Fact and fiction may well have been confused, for the message was far more important than historical detail. What evolved are the Gospel stories we use today that are attributed to Matthew, Mark, Luke, and John.

Jesus was born and lived most of his life in Palestine—the traditional land of Israel as defined in the Jewish scriptures. In the first century B.C., Palestine was divided into three provinces—Judea, Galilee, and Samaria—all of which were under Roman rule.

Galilee, the most northern of the three provinces, was the principal setting for Jesus' life, especially the area around its lake, commonly known as the Sea of Galilee. His hometown of Nazareth was a small and insignificant village—a satellite of the larger, more cosmopolitan city of Sepphoris, which was just an hour's walk away.

During Jesus' lifetime Galilee was governed by King Herod the Great (37–4 B.C.) and then afterward his son, the tetrarch Herod Antipas (4 B.C.–39 A.D.), both ruling as prefects of Rome.

The most important city in Palestine, then as now, was Jerusalem. Well away from the main trade routes and areas of population, Jerusalem was not a great economic center but was primarily a religious and political capital and was filled with people from all over the known world. Herod the Great had undertaken some major building projects in the city, and the most notable was the rebuilding of the Temple, the central focus for Jewish pilgrimage and celebrations. The significance of Jerusalem went far beyond its geography, for it symbolized a place of hope, where God and humanity would dwell together.

Jesus was presumed to be the realization of this dream. As he entered manhood and began to preach, his message to humanity clearly declared that the kingdom of God was at hand. Those who drew close to him, he said, would experience and know it.

The Annunciation

It is Luke who best tells the story of Jesus' birth. He begins by saying that the angel Gabriel was sent from God to a city of Galilee called Nazareth, to a virgin betrothed to a man whose name was Joseph, of the house of David; and the virgin's name was Mary. When Gabriel appeared he greeted Mary with the words, "Hail, O favored one, the Lord is with you! Blessed you are among women." Mary was troubled, and wondered what was happening. Gabriel continued, "Do not be afraid, for you have found favor with God. You will conceive in your womb and bear a son, and you will call him Jesus. He will be great, and will be called the Son of the Most High; and the Lord God will give to him the throne of his father David, and he will reign over the house of Jacob forever; and there will be no end to his kingdom."

"How can this be," questioned Mary, "since I have not been with any man?"

Gabriel answered that through the greatest of mysteries, Mary would conceive the Son of God with the Holy Spirit. Hearing this Mary bowed her head and said, "I am the servant of the Lord; let it be as you have said." With this, the angel departed.

Zechariah and Elizabeth

About six months previous to the annunciation, Mary's cousin Elizabeth and her husband Zechariah also miraculously conceived a child. They were an old but childless couple who lived in the hills of Judea. According to Jewish beliefs at the time, infertility was an indication of God's displeasure and Elizabeth lived under the terrible stigma of divine reproach for her barrenness.

Zechariah was a priest. One day while he was in the Temple, an angel appeared before him and announced that his wife would give birth to a son whose name was to be John. John would become a prophet and win many Jews back to God while preparing the way for the coming Messiah.

The angel said, "I am Gabriel, and I have been sent to tell you this and also to say that you will be struck dumb, and you will not able to speak until everything I told you has come to pass."

When Zecharias left the temple, he went up to a crowd of people who were waiting for him. They understood that he had seen a vision in the Temple for he motioned to them with his hands, but he could tell them nothing.

The Visitation

Mary decided to visit her cousin Elizabeth who lived in a small town near Jerusalem. Upon entering the house she called out Elizabeth's name and ran to embrace her. As she did so the child in Elizabeth's womb leaped as if in recognition of the child that Mary carried. Elizabeth was filled with wonder and, immediately understanding what had happened, she exclaimed, "Blessed you are among women, and blessed is the fruit of your womb. How is it that the mother of my Lord has come to visit me? I don't understand—but at the sound of your voice, the child in my womb has leaped for joy."

Mary, overcome by wonder and awe, burst into song:

> *My soul praises the Lord,*
> *and my spirit rejoices in God my Savior*
> *for he has seen the humility of*
> *his handmaiden. From henceforth*
> *all generations will call me blessed*
> *because he that is mighty has done wonderful*
> *things through me. O holy is his name!*

Joseph and Mary Travel to Bethlehem

Although it has not been born out in historical records, Luke tells us that a decree went out from Caesar Augustus, Emperor of Rome, ordering a census to be taken in Palestine, in order to facilitate the collection of taxes: Every male in the land was to return to the city of his birth and have his name registered. It was due to this decree that Joseph took Mary out of Nazareth to Bethlehem.

Bethlehem is situated about six miles south of Jerusalem, and perhaps a hundred miles from Nazareth. It had been the birthplace, many centuries earlier, of the great king David who united the tribes of Israel and made Jerusalem the capital. He was greatly loved as a poet-singer and played upon a lyre. Yahweh, the Jewish God, had proclaimed through a prophet that David's lineage would deliver the people of Israel from their suffering. Since that time, there had been many prophecies regarding the coming Messiah and the people of Israel eagerly awaited his birth.

The word "messiah" is derived from an older word meaning "anointed" and was sometimes used as another word for "king." The prophet Micah had said specifically that the Messiah would come from Bethlehem.

The Nativity

Heavy with child and very tired, Mary arrived in Bethlehem with Joseph. He searched for a place to stay but because of the census the town was filled with visitors. Finding no place to stay, they made their way to an empty stable or small cave in the nearby hillside. There they settled in a dry corner and Mary gave birth to her first-born son.

She wrapped the babe in swaddling clothes and laid him in a manger. Exhausted and greatly relieved, Mary and Joseph gave thanks to God, and some time later, their hearts filled with gratitude, they fell asleep.

Divinely conceived and successfully delivered, the child was protected by a heavenly host of angels. Sheltered by the warmth of nearby animals with whom they shared their abode, the holy family rested. When the child was forty days old, Joseph and Mary would take him to Jerusalem for religious rites that were necessary under Jewish custom.

The Shepherds

Meanwhile, in nearby fields there were some shepherds watching over their flocks. Suddenly an angel appeared before them. The shepherds were terrified, but the angel put them at ease and said to them, "Fear not; for I bring you good tidings of great joy for all people."

As the shepherds began to relax and quiet down, the angel continued, proclaiming the wonderful news that "Unto you is born this day, in the city of David, a Savior who is Christ the Lord. And this shall be a sign unto you: You will find the child wrapped in swaddling clothes, lying in a manger."

When the angels had disappeared the shepherds decided to hurry to Bethlehem to see what had happened there. When they arrived they found Mary and Joseph with their child lying in a manger.

After bestowing their best wishes upon the child, the shepherds left and went back to their village. They began to talk of what had happened, and all those who heard their tale were fascinated by what they said. Word of what had happened spread quickly.

Presentation in the Temple

When Jesus was forty days old, Mary and Joseph took him to the Temple in Jerusalem for customary religious rites. As an offering of purification for Mary, two turtledoves were sacrificed.

At the temple there was a man named Simeon who had earlier heard in a vision that he would not die until he had set eyes on the Messiah. Simeon was present at the ceremony with Jesus and his parents. Once it was over, he took the child in his arms and prayed, "Master, let your servant go in peace. As You promised, my eyes have seen the salvation—a light of revelation and glory for your people Israel." Mary and Joseph stood by and Simeon blessed them and then said quietly to Mary, "Your son is destined to be opposed. There are those who will want to destroy him, and with this a sword will pierce your soul—but through your sorrow the hearts of many will be opened."

Soon after this a prophetess named Anna, a widow who served in the Temple, came forward and also gave thanks. She too picked up the child and spoke of the coming redemption of mankind through his blessedness.

The Three Wise Men

The Gospel of Matthew recounts the story of the three wise men who came to Jerusalem from the East with news of a newborn child who was to become the King of the Jews. They reached the court of Herod the Great and when they were asked for details they answered that they had seen his star in the night sky and that they had come to worship him.

When Herod heard this, he was troubled and he gathered his chief priests and demanded that they tell him where the child was. The priests told Herod that the prophets of old had foretold that the child would be born in Bethlehem.

Herod then called the wise men and asked them to go to Bethlehem and to find the child. "When you have found him, bring word to me that I too may go and worship him." With this the wise men left and as they went to Bethlehem, a bright star guided them to the place where the young child was.

They entered the stable, and finding the child and his mother, Mary, they fell to their knees in prayer. Then they opened up the treasures they had brought and presented the child with gifts of gold, frankincense, and myrrh.

The Flight into Egypt

Warned by God in a dream that they should not return to Herod, the wise men went back to their own country by another route. After they had left, an angel appeared to Joseph in a dream and told him to get up and take the young child and his mother with him. "Go to Egypt and wait there until I bring word to you, for Herod will seek the child out and will destroy him." So the family headed towards the sea and took a coastal road to the Nile Valley.

During the previous centuries, following the exodus out of Egypt under Moses, the peoples of Israel and Egypt had settled into a peaceful relationship. Eventually a growing number of Jews had moved to Egypt to settle, and the city of Alexandria became one of the most respected centers of Jewish learning.

We do not know where in Egypt the family settled, but Joseph and Mary would certainly have found a safe haven there as they waited for the time when Herod would cease to be a threat to their child. Coptic Christians of Egypt still worship a gigantic sycamore that stands in a garden on the edge of ancient Heliopolis, a few miles from Cairo where they may have lived.

Herod's Massacre

When the wise men failed to return to his court Herod realized he had been betrayed and he was furious. He ordered his troops to raid Bethlehem and its environs and to slay all the male children who were two years old or younger. It was Herod's intention to kill the newborn "King" in this massacre of innocent children.

The soldiers carried out their orders, leaving a trail of terror among the families of Bethlehem. A great mourning was taken up throughout the land. It is known as the Lament of Rachel and is the cry of women who could not be comforted, weeping for their children.

Although the historical records reveal no actual slaughter of children by Herod, we do know that he, in order to consolidate his rule over Judea, harshly punished those who opposed him and richly rewarded those who supported him. He ordered the murder of his wife, and all male relatives including some of his own children in order to leave no rival for his throne. His death in 4 B.C. was a signal for the eruption of fierce resentments that had accumulated during his reign. Revolt and tension spread throughout the country.

Childhood of Jesus

Herod died, and in his will he bequeathed the southern part of Palestine to his son Archaelaus, and the title of tetrarch (governor) along with the northern areas he gave to another son, Herod Antipas.

After Herod's death an angel appeared in a dream to Joseph and told him to take the young child and his mother, and to return to Israel. Feeling somewhat fearful of the new ruler of Bethlehem Joseph decided to settle in Nazareth, thus fulfilling an old prophecy that the Messiah would be a Nazarene.

There is a thirty-year gap between the accounts of Jesus' birth and the beginning of his ministry. The only information we have from the Gospels about his early years comes from the Gospel of Luke where we are told that the child grew and became strong and that he was filled with wisdom and the grace of God. During his youth it is possible that he played with his cousin John, the son of Elizabeth, along with his brothers Jacob, Joseph, Judas, Simon and his sisters Melcha and Escha. There are stories in the Apocrypha that tell of childhood pranks and bizarre miracles such as one in which he had children who played tricks on him put to death and then restored to life.

Jesus in the Temple

A single event in the Gospel of Luke concerning Jesus' childhood tells of the twelve-year-old boy being taken to the Jerusalem Temple. His parents made the journey to Jerusalem every year for the feast of Passover, along with many other people from around the countryside.

Having set out on the return journey, Mary and Joseph traveled for the better part of a day before they realized that the child Jesus was nowhere to be found. They returned to the capital and spent three frantic days looking for him before they finally found him in the Temple, sitting in the midst of priests and learned men, listening to them and asking questions. The men were clearly astonished at the depth of his understanding.

Mary asked Jesus what had happened and why he had not returned with them. He answered her with the question: "Do you wish me not to do my Father's business?"

Not understanding this response, Mary turned the strange words over in her heart as the family returned to Nazareth.

John the Baptist Prepares the Way

Following the deaths of his parents, John grew up in the desert of Judea. He later moved to the wilderness lands east of the Jordan River where he began to preach and to practice the ritual of baptism. Like prophets who had gone before him, John wore camel skins and fed on locusts and wild honey.

The essence of John's message was that lineal descent from Abraham would not guarantee salvation, and that a symbolic act of renunciation was necessary. He also called for repentance in preparation for the coming Day of Judgment.

John was very outspoken and the young Jesus was certainly inspired by him. It is likely that he was a disciple of John's before he began his own ministry.

John the Forerunner, as he is sometimes called, fulfilled his father's prophecy that he would prepare the way for the coming Messiah. Large crowds came to him for baptism in the Jordan river and thought that he might be the Messiah, but John told them, "After me will come one more powerful than I—a man whose sandals I am not worthy to touch. I baptize you with water, but he will baptize you with the Holy Spirit."

The Baptism of Jesus

One day Jesus came to the Jordan to be baptized by John. We have not been told in the Gospels where he came from or what he had been doing in preparation, but it is clear that by this time he was about thirty years old and that he was well acquainted with the scriptures. He must have delved deeply into questions of spiritual substance and studied with various teachers.

John, when he saw Jesus approaching, knew for certain that the man who stood before him was the one whose coming he had announced. "Behold the Lamb of God, who will take away the sins of the world," he said. He then tried to stop Jesus from coming to him, saying, "It is I who needs to be baptized by you. Why do you come to me?" Jesus simply replied that it was necessary.

After the baptism, Jesus rose up and walked toward the bank of the river. The heavens seemed to open up, and John saw the Spirit of God descend like a dove to light on Jesus. A voice rang out and said, "This is my Son, whom I love; with him I am well pleased."

The Temptation in the Wilderness

After his baptism Jesus retired to the wilderness of the desert for forty days of deep meditation and a cleansing of his soul that would prepare him for his mission. During this period he lived through the deepest and darkest temptations of the body and mind from which he emerged with a spirit that was as indomitable as it was clear and true. Luke described the temptations in the desert as a series of trials in which Jesus was visited by the devil who challenged him in different ways. He first tried to get Jesus to turn stones to bread, but Jesus replied that turning stones to bread had no real significance. "Man does not live by bread alone, but by the word of God."

Then the devil set him on a pinnacle and tried to tempt him again. "If you are the Son of God, cast yourself down, for it is written that God will protect you." To this Jesus replied that he would not betray his trust in God nor would his soul be tempted by the devil's antics.

Finally the devil took him up a mountain, and told him he would be lord of all he saw if he would turn away from God. To this Jesus replied that he worshiped only one God, "And him only will I serve."

The Death of John the Baptist

At this time Galilee was governed by Herod Antipas, the son of Herod the Great. John the Baptist had spoken out against Antipas, condemning him for marrying his brother's wife, Herodias. She was furious at this public announcement and wanted to have John killed, but Antipas was afraid. He knew of John's reputation as a holy man and simply had him arrested and put into prison.

At his birthday celebration Herod gave a banquet for the nobles of his court, and it was during this banquet that Herodias' daughter, Salome, came in and danced. She so delighted Herod that he promised to give her anything she wanted. The girl went to speak with her mother and returned to Herod saying, "I want the head of John the Baptist." Unable to go back on his word, Herod sent one of his bodyguards to the prison with orders to bring back John's head, and sometime later, the prophet's head was brought in on a dish and presented to Salome who gave it to her mother Herodias.

When John's disciples heard about his terrible death, they came and took the body away and laid it in a tomb. John the Forerunner had paid the ultimate price for speaking out in truth against the authorities.

The Calling of the First Disciples

After returning from the temptations in the wilderness, Jesus began teaching in Nazareth where he may have conducted a ministry of baptism similar to that of John the Baptist. He went into the synagogues to preach, and after a while began to speak in the open air, reaching out to people rather than waiting for them to come to him.

After John had been put in prison, political tensions grew and Jesus went to Capernaum, a town on the shore of the Sea of Galilee, where he began to gather his disciples. There were many who were captivated by his words and his presence and were so touched that they left their homes behind and followed him closely, learning great lessons by immersing themselves in his presence.

Andrew and his brother Simon were fishermen. They were casting their nets into the Sea of Galilee, when Jesus approached them and said, "Come, follow me." They immediately put down their nets and followed him. Jesus went a little farther and saw James and his brother John, also fishermen. He called them too, and they left their father behind in the boat with their nets, and followed Jesus.

The Miracle of Feeding

People began to gather in small groups to listen to Jesus, and as word of his wonderful presence began to spread, the groups grew in size. People began to see him as John's natural successor and also as the potential new Messiah they so badly needed in the face of Roman oppression.

One day a crowd of perhaps five thousand people had gathered, and while Jesus spoke to them, the hours passed. When evening approached, some of the disciples came to him to say that it was getting late. They suggested that the people might need to go into the local villages and buy themselves food, but Jesus said that they do not need to go away. "Give them some food." The disciples replied that they had only five loaves of bread and two fish.

So Jesus told the crowd to sit down on the grass. He took the fish and the loaves of bread and, looking to heaven, blessed the food. He then took the bread and began to break it into pieces, which he gave to his disciples. They, in turn, distributed the food to the crowds. Everyone was fed and was satisfied, and at the end of the meal twelve baskets of leftovers were gathered.

The Teachings

For three years Jesus traveled up and down the countryside, teaching about the kingdom of God, about love and compassion, and about true life. Sometimes he taught in plain words, sometimes in obscure, mysterious parables, and sometimes in direct argument and confrontation with those who challenged him.

Jesus did not call on people to leave the world and to go into the wilderness or the mountains. He sought them in their villages and took part in their ordinary lives. He presented them with parables and stories through which they could see the true strength and the power of trusting in God in this world, in the present moment.

Jesus taught not only with the words, he also taught through miracles of healing and acts of compassion. He healed the body and he healed the spirit. He restored sight to the blind and health to the ailing. He even brought the dead back to life. The miracles of Jesus reflected the miracles of everyday life and he taught people to love and to trust each other.

He based his teaching upon the Jewish scriptures—with which he was fully familiar and which he loved dearly. He augmented these teachings with his own personal understanding, an understanding born of his unique relationship with God.

Common people responded to the teachings of Jesus. They loved and trusted him and he spoke to them of their spiritual heritage in a way that made it alive for them—relating it to their own direct experiences. He taught them not to judge each other, and brought them out of the past and into the present moment. He showed them, through examples drawn from their own lives, ways in which they could find peace, joy, and greater happiness in life.

There are many ways to interpret the teachings of Jesus for he spoke on many levels. Underneath the surface of every tale was a lesson that could be easily remembered. Jesus avoided subtle and elaborate descriptions and taught with disarming simplicity. He conveyed profound and complex concepts in a manner that could be easily grasped. With masterful dedication to his mission, Jesus reached out and touched the hearts of humankind.

.

The Disciples

When Jesus began teaching, many men and women gathered around him. He called upon some of them to abandon their homes for a while and to join him in his wanderings. These became his close disciples. Whatever the cost, their discipleship was first. Through absolute devotion they imbibed a sense of who he was. Through real absorption in his presence they had glimpses of the experiences that gave meaning to his actions and his words.

The word "disciple" literally means "pupil" or "learner." Jesus' disciples stayed close to him. They watched and listened to him continuously and learned from him in a most experiential way.

Jesus taught them in a variety of ways. He loved the Jewish scriptures, and he taught from them, and his love gave new meaning to the words. He had immense respect for the ancient prophets, and he breathed energy into their sayings and brought their teachings to life. He prayed with his disciples while they entered into the sacred pulse of creation. He loved his disciples, and in his love for them they bathed in a new understanding that carried them to an ever deeper and ever more immediate experience of the divine love of God.

The Commandments

One day a teacher of the Jewish law entered into a conversation Jesus was having and asked, "Of all the commandments, which is the most important?"

Jesus answered, "The first is 'the Lord our God is one; you shall love the Lord your God with all your heart, and with all your soul, and with all your mind, and with all your strength.' The second is this, 'You shall love your neighbor as yourself.' There is no commandment greater than these."

Love, the essence of Jesus' teaching, was translated into every word and action of his ministry. Love, trust, and service to God and all creation were the basic principles that guided his every action.

"If you love those who love you, what credit is that to you? Even sinners love those who love them. If you give to those from whom you expect repayment, what is your reward? Love your enemies. Do good to them and give to them without expecting any return. Then your rewards will be great. Be merciful, just as your Father is merciful." Love is the key, he said. Love alone will transform desire and greed, but you will know love only if you can practice it.

God the Father

The concept of God as father is central to the life and teaching of Jesus. It derives from the Hebrew scriptures where God is sometimes described as the Father of the Israelite nation.

Jesus had an intimate and personal relationship with God. He was the Son. In addressing God, the Father, Jesus often used the word *Abba*, an Aramaic word that carried the sense of familiarity that a young child would have with a parent. To Jesus, God was the caretaker, the nonjudgemental arbitrator who loves all things equally. "Are not five sparrows sold for two pennies? Yet not one of them is forgotten by God."

Jesus described a Father who was forgiving and merciful. "He causes the sun to rise on both evil and good, and sends rain on the righteous and the unrighteous alike." He described a Father who was present in every moment and far more magnificent than the mind of humankind can possibly comprehend.

The Kingdom of God

The Pharisees were one of the religious groups in Palestine in the time of Jesus. They interpreted the scriptures in such a way that its meanings could be applied to everyday life and were known for their love of debate and for keeping alive the tradition of meditation and contemplation of the scriptures. They believed in resurrection and in future rewards and punishments.

One day a Pharisee asked Jesus when the kingdom of God would come. Jesus replied, "The kingdom of God will not come as a result of what you do or think, nor will it be announced to you. The kingdom of God is within you."

The theme of the kingdom of God was a principal theme of Jesus' message. He spoke of God as reigning over all things and the kingdom as a divine state that is not limited in time or place. His claim to speak on behalf of the kingdom of God was not unfounded. The truth he spoke was born of a direct experience of God within. He was the Son of God. Jesus had awakened to a unique and divine relationship that exists between the soul, the human heart, and God.

Jesus Walks on Water

After the miracle in which Jesus fed the large crowd with five loaves of bread and a few fish, people were quite excited, for they saw in the miracle a sign of his messianic powers and insisted on calling him their king. Jesus, however, wanted nothing to do with such royal titles and withdrew from their hysteria, sending his disciples back across the Sea of Galilee.

He went up the mountain by himself to pray. When he came down the disciples were still at sea and he went out to see them, walking upon the water. When they saw him they were quite alarmed, and cried out in fear, thinking he was a ghost. Jesus spoke to them saying, "It is I, do not be afraid."

Peter called him and said, "Lord, if it is you, ask me to come to you." So Jesus did, and Peter got out of the boat and walked on the water to meet Jesus. Suddenly, not believing what he was doing, he panicked and started to falter. As he began to sink he cried out, "Lord, save me!"

Jesus at once stretched out his hand and took hold of Peter, saying to him, "O you of little faith, why did you doubt?"

The Marriage at Cana

In the tiny village of Cana, not far from Nazareth, Jesus' mother, Mary, went to a wedding feast to which Jesus and his disciples had also been invited. At a point when the feast was winding down Mary noticed that the wine was gone and she leaned over to Jesus and told him.

"Dear woman, why do you tell me?" he said. "My time has not yet come."

Mary went over to the servants and whispered, "Do whatever he tells you."

Nearby stood six water jars. Jesus soon went over and told the servants to fill them, and so they did. Then he told them to take some of the water and give it to the master of the banquet. This they also did, and when the master tasted the wine he was so impressed by its sweet taste that he called the bridegroom aside and complemented him on the fine wine.

There is a beautiful wisdom in Mary's words to the servants, "Do whatever he tells you." They have been remembered as a command to recognize Jesus as the man whose presence as a teacher was miraculous.

Sermon on the Mount

Jesus had spent a night in prayer. The next morning he gathered his disciples together and spoke to them at length about his teachings.

Blessed are those who know nothing, for theirs is the kingdom of heaven.
Blessed are those who grieve, for they will be comforted.
Blessed are those who hunger for righteousness, for they will be filled.
Blessed are the pure in heart, for they will see God.
Blessed are the peacemakers, for they will be called sons of God.

He went on to give examples of how the righteous would behave. He spoke of strength and humility, and the ability to discern right from wrong and the true from the untrue. "The person who hears these words of mine and puts them into practice is like a wise person who builds a house on rock. When the rain comes and the winds blow and beat against the house, it doesn't fall because its foundation is solid. The person who hears these words and does not put them into practice is foolish and like the person who builds his house on sand. When the rain comes and the winds blow and beat against that house, it falls down with a great crash."

Prayer

Jesus taught the disciples about prayer: "When you pray, do not be like the hypocrite who loves to pray standing on the street corners where he can be seen by others. When you pray, go inside, be alone, and pray to your Father, who is unseen. Your Father, knows the secrets of your heart, and will reward you. When you pray, do not babble like an idiot who thinks he will be listened to because of his many words. Be sincere. Your Father knows your needs." And he taught the disciples the following prayer:

Our Father in heaven,
hallowed is your name.
May your kingdom come,
may your will be done
on earth as it is in heaven.
Give us today our daily bread.
Forgive us our wrongs,
as we also have forgiven those who have wronged us.
And lead us not into temptation,
but deliver us from evil.

Nicodemus Visits Jesus

Jesus' fame spread as he taught and healed the common people and he soon came to the attention of the Sanhedrin, the body of religious authorities who governed the religious life of the nation. The Sanhedrin was composed of a high priest, a number of leading priests and experts in the law, and prominent members of two groups called Pharisees and Sadduccees. The Roman government allowed this group to decide on most religious and civil matters.

One night a member of the Sanhedrin, a Pharisee named Nicodemus, sought Jesus out. It is not known whether he was sent by the Sanhedrin or whether he came out of personal curiosity, but he asked Jesus about his teachings concerning the kingdom of heaven.

Jesus explained to him that he spoke only from the truth of his own experience and that no one enters the kingdom of heaven unless he lives in both the world of the flesh and the world of the spirit. The light of truth shines in this world, but many people prefer darkness and do not move towards light because they fear their deeds will be exposed. Those who are not afraid to stand in the light are those who know that God is alive inside of them.

Parable of the Sower

Jesus often spoke through parables, relating specific teachings through images that were easily understood. He once likened himself to a sower.

"When he sows, some seeds fall by the wayside and birds come and devour them up. Some seeds fall on stony ground where there is not much earth and these seeds sprout, but when the sun comes out, the sprouts are scorched. Some seeds fall among thorns which grow up and choke the sprouts so that they yield no fruit. And some seeds fall on fertile earth where they grow strong and yield good fruit, and as they grow their fruit increases."

When Jesus was alone, the disciples came to him and asked about the meaning of the parable. He was surprised they did not understand, and explained: "The seeds are like my words. There are some that land on the wayside and when they have been heard, Satan comes immediately, and turns them around. Some words land on stony ground and are received with gladness, but when trouble comes people forget what they have heard. Some are sown among thorns where people hear them, but are choked by lust. Some words land on fertile ground, where they are well received and grow strong and bear fine fruit.

The Woman Taken in Adultery

One morning as Jesus was teaching in the Temple courtyard some religious leaders forcibly brought a woman through the crowd to him. They told him that the woman was guilty of adultery and according to their interpretation of the law she deserved to be stoned to death.

Jesus did not fall into their trap. He squatted down on his heels and, without a word, began writing on the ground with his finger. They continued to press him for a judgment, repeating over and over that the law called for her death. Eventually Jesus stood up and looked the men in the eye, saying, "He that is without sin amongst you, let him throw the first stone." He stooped down again and continued looking at the ground and writing with his finger. One by one, the men walked away, until only Jesus and the woman were left.

What happened?" he asked her. "Has no one accused you?"

"No, Lord," she said.

"Neither do I," he said. "Go and sin no more."

The House of a Pharisee

Jesus was invited to dine at the house of a Pharisee. A woman in the town, upon learning that he was there, brought an alabaster jar of ointment. She bathed his feet with her tears, and wiped them with her hair. Then she kissed his feet, and anointed them with the ointment. The Pharisee thought this was strange because the woman was known to be a sinner. He thought that if Jesus were really a prophet, surely he would know who and what manner of woman she was. Jesus looked at him and understanding his thoughts said, "A certain money lender had two debtors; one owed five hundred coins, the other fifty. As they had no means of paying, he forgave them both. Which of them, therefore, will love the man more?"

"I came into your house and you gave me no water for my feet; but this woman has bathed my feet with tears. Therefore her sins, many as they are, shall be forgiven her, because she has loved much. Then he turned to the woman and said, "Your faith has saved you. Go in peace."

The men who were sitting at the Pharisee's table looked at each other and asked, "Who is this man, who thinks he can forgive another's sin?"

Healing Miracles

As he taught Jesus also healed, touching both body and spirit with his hands. Throughout the Gospel stories he showed immense compassion for those burdened by pain—moral, spiritual, and physical. He saw that the mystery of suffering was deep at the root of human existence, and inseparable from sin and estrangement from God.

He once said, "The blind receive sight, the lame walk, those who have leprosy are cured, the deaf hear, the dead are raised, and the good news is preached to the poor. Blessed are those who listen."

One day some men brought a paralyzed friend to Jesus. Dramatically they lifted tiles from the roof of the house in which Jesus was teaching and let their friend down by ropes until he lay at Jesus' feet. The crowd was astonished at this and even more when Jesus forgave the man his sins. The religious teachers that were present accused him of blaspheming, saying that only God can forgive a person's sins. "Which is easier," Jesus asked them, "to forgive sins or to heal the body?" He then ordered the man to take up his bed and walk away—which he did.

The Woman at the Well

Jesus and his disciples were traveling through Samaria, a region most Jews avoided, since Jews and Samaritans distrusted each other. Near the town of Sychar he sent his disciples ahead to buy some food and, hot and tired, he sat down by a well. While he was resting a woman came to draw water. When Jesus asked her for a drink, she was surprised and asked how it was that he, a Jew, would deign to speak with a Samaritan woman.

He replied that if she only knew who he was, she would ask him for a drink of living water. She pointed out that he had no bucket and asked where he would get living water. He explained that living water was new life surging in the soul and would bring eternal life. She asked him for some and he told her to call her husband. The woman said she was not married. Jesus said that she was not presently married, but that she had had five husbands in the past.

Astounded that he knew so much about her the woman asked Jesus to tell her where God should be worshiped—in Jerusalem as the Jews said or on Mount Gerizim as the Samaritans insisted. Jesus explained that it isn't where you worship, but how you worship that matters.

Lazarus

Due to growing opposition Jesus moved to a town east of the Jordan River but upon learning that his friend Lazarus was very sick he went to Bethany to visit him. When he arrived he found that Lazarus had died four days earlier and seeing the sorrow of his sisters at the loss of their brother, Jesus wept and attempted in vain to comfort them. He asked to be taken to Lazarus' tomb where a large crowd had gathered to mourn. Jesus ordered the stone to be rolled away from the tomb's entrance and called out, "Lazarus, come forth!" As the crowd watched breathlessly, the shape of a man wrapped in burial clothes walked toward them.

After the dramatic raising of Lazarus some people hurried to Jerusalem to report the miracle to the Sanhedrin who held an emergency meeting and plotted to have Jesus killed as soon as possible. They were worried about the growing crowds of people who believed that Jesus was the Messiah. Some of the members of the Sanhedrin were afraid that the Romans might decide to destroy the Jewish nation in order to retain their power. Caiaphas, the high priest, summed the situation up saying, "It is better that one man should die for the people, than that the whole should perish."

The Transfiguration

Jesus took Peter, James, and John to the top of a high mountain where they were all alone. He knelt down to pray and as the three disciples struggled to keep their eyes open, he was transformed into light.

Before their eyes his whole appearance changed and he radiated an inner glow. Two men suddenly appeared with him, also alive with light—Moses and Elijah—representing the law and the prophets of Israel's history. The three luminous figures talked together about Jesus' imminent death in Jerusalem.

Suddenly they were surrounded by a cloud, and from within this cloud the disciples heard a voice say, "This is my beloved son: Listen to him." Then, as suddenly as they had appeared, Moses and Elijah vanished. Looking around the disciples saw only Jesus.

As they descended the mountain, Jesus insisted that the disciples tell no one what they had seen until he had risen from the dead. They kept the matter to themselves and tried to figure out what he meant by "risen from the dead."

Jesus Predicts His Death

As problems with the authorities developed, Jesus explained to his disciples that he must go to Jerusalem where he would suffer many things at the hands of the elders, chief priests, and Romans. He said he would be killed and on the third day be raised to life.

Peter took him aside and insisted to the contrary. "Never, Lord!" he said. "This shall never happen to you!"

Jesus turned and told Peter that he must try to understand the deeper meaning of things, otherwise he would undermine the teachings. Then he turned to his disciples, "If anyone wants to come after me, he must deny himself and take up his own cross and follow me. For whoever wants to save his life will lose it, but whoever loses his life for me will find it. What good will come to a person who gains the whole world, if he forfeits his soul? And what can a man give in exchange for his soul?"

"The Son of Man is coming to his Father's glory. I tell you, some of who stand here with me today will live to see the Son of Man in his kingdom."

The Final Days

The stories about the last days of Jesus' life are collectively known as the Passion. The details of the events are laden with wonderful complexities, both historic and spiritual, and have become firmly imprinted in our collective mind. Contained in these stories lie all the themes that made Jesus' life so remarkable—his extraordinary relationship with God the Father, the simplicity of his teachings, and his call to enter the kingdom of heaven. Essentially a mystery that cannot be comprehended by the mind alone, the events of the final days express some of the great paradoxes of spiritual life.

It is said in many traditions that we must die in order to be reborn in heaven. Likewise it is known to all who travel into the uncharted regions of the inner world that to know ourselves we must enter into the kingdom of eternal life. Real life is known only in the present moment through a process of dying to the ego and realizing the eternity of here and now. This state is often likened to awakening and the crucifixion of Jesus marks his own final awakening into the absolute kingdom of God.

In early Christian art Jesus was often depicted as a lamb, a symbol that probably derived from the Passover lamb of Jewish tradition. The Gospel of John speaks of Jesus as the lamb that takes away the sins of the world, and refers to the crucifixion of Jesus as a parallel to the ceremonial killing of the lamb that is eaten at Passover.

Sacrifice has always been a central theme of spiritual growth—where temporal life is lived with such heartfulness that it is transformed into an experience of eternal life. Just as at every meal, we transform matter into energy, so the sacrificial lamb is a symbol of our desire to transform ourselves.

The events of the final days of Jesus make up a powerful story of transformation and ultimate acceptance of the will of God. Betrayal, confusion, fear, and misunderstanding are essential elements. They are qualities that we must all wrestle with during our own growth and transformation. All the episodes that are contained in the stories on the following pages live within each one of us. The characters that play out the Passion can be seen as different aspects of ourselves. The great temptation of the human predicament is to fall asleep, like Jesus' disciples so often did, and to miss the beauty of the moment.

Triumphal Entry into Jerusalem

It is not clear from reports in the Gospels how long the Galillean ministry of Jesus lasted. Based on the details that are described, scholars assume it was about a year. The Gospels also present varied accounts of the period in which Jesus and his disciples journeyed to Jerusalem but in all of them, a darkening shadow was cast by Jesus' predictions of the Passion. He told them he would be delivered into the hands of enemies and that they would condemn him to death. He would be mocked, scourged, and spat upon, and finally he would be killed. On the third day, he said, he would rise again.

Jesus was in Bethany shortly after the miracle of raising Lazarus from the dead. It was the week before Passover and he decided to go to Jerusalem for the feast. Two of his disciples had found a donkey for him to ride upon and as the group began the short walk into the city, excitement grew. People cried out in joy. Some spread clothes on the road in front of him and others cut palm branches from nearby trees, which they laid down in an act of homage. A chant welled up as they approached the city: "Hosanna to the son of David, Blessed is he that comes in the name of the Lord; Hosanna in the highest."

The Cleansing of the Temple

Shortly after his arrival in Jerusalem a conflict with the religious authorities culminated in the series of events that was to lead to his death. Having condemned the corrupt practices of certain priests, he now attacked the commercialization of the sacrificial system.

As he walked through the sacred Temple court he saw that it had been transformed into a commercial operation. Priests insisted upon the use of specially created "Temple money" as the sole means of exchange in the Temple grounds and they profited enormously from a high rate of exchange when these coins were purchased. Further, they had decreed that sacrificial animals could only be purchased on Temple grounds, and for these they set their own prices.

Animals, moneychangers, and pilgrims jammed the court, and the travesties that went on so offended Jesus that he made a whip and flailed it about himself, turning over the tables of the moneychangers and disrupting the sale of animals. In a loud voice he cried out that it is written in the scriptures that "the Temple is a house of prayer—but you have made it a den of thieves."

The Last Supper

Because of the large crowds that followed him everywhere, Jesus made secret arrangements to celebrate the Passover meal alone with his disciples in the room of a private home. Quietly and unnoticed in the dusk of the feast, Jesus and his disciples found their way into the room. Passover, a festival celebrating the exodus of the Hebrews from Egypt, begins with the breaking of bread.

At the height of the meal Jesus added to the symbolic elements that were spoken to at Passover by taking the bread. He gave thanks and broke it, and gave it to his disciples, saying, "Take, eat. This is my body."

Then he took a cup of wine, gave thanks and offered it to them, saying, "This is my blood of the new testament, which is shed for many. I will not drink the fruit of the vine again until that day when I drink it in the kingdom of God."

As the disciples were eagerly picturing themselves as leaders in the new kingdom, they began quarreling about which one would be the greatest. Jesus rebuked them saying that the chief among them was to be the servant of all, since his kingdom was not at all like the kingdoms of the world.

Washing of the Feet

Later in the evening Jesus took off his outer robe and wrapped a towel around his waist. Then he poured water into a basin and began to wash the feet of his disciples. When he came to Peter, Peter voiced his upset at seeing Jesus so humbled. Jesus explained that the ways of a teacher are often mysterious and that a disciple should remain as open as possible to the master's teachings even if he cannot understand them.

After he had finished washing their feet, Jesus sat down and said to his disciples, "As I have washed your feet, you should wash the feet of each other. Remember, the servant is not greater than his lord; nor is he that is sent greater than he that sent him." He went on to say that he would be with them always but indicated that he would be leaving them soon. Peter asked where he was going, "I will follow you anywhere. I will lay down my life for you."

In a quiet voice Jesus said that all the followers would desert him and to Peter he said, "Before the morning cock crows, you will have denied me three times."

Judas Iscariot

Of the twelve disciples, there was one who was to betray Jesus that night. His devotion had turned sour, and Judas Iscariot sold his heart for thirty pieces of silver. Jesus was aware of Judas' treacherous intention and in the middle of the symbolic meal he told Judas to go and do what was in his mind to do. The others thought that Jesus had merely sent Judas out on an errand but Judas had made a deal with the authorities that he would let them know when it was safe to seize Jesus.

A few days later, feeling sorry for what he had done, Judas went to the Jewish priests with the money they had given him and said, "I have sinned. I have betrayed innocent blood." But they refused to take the money back.

Judas threw down the pieces of silver and went and hanged himself. The priests picked up the coins and agreed that it would not be right to put the money into the treasury because it was the price of blood. So they went and bought a potter's field to bury strangers in. The name of this field was later called "Haceldama" or "Field of Blood."

Agony in the Garden

Jesus and the remaining eleven disciples sang a hymn before setting out in the dark for an olive grove on a nearby mountain. Part way up to the Mount of Olives they stopped at a quiet place known as the Garden of Gethsemane. Jesus asked eight of the disciples to stay near the entrance and he took Peter, James, and John into the garden with him. He asked them to keep watch and to pray while he went to a spot where he could be alone, telling them his heart was full of sorrow. "Stop here and stay awake," he said. He went deeper into the garden and fell to the ground in prayer. There he wrestled with his own will and the will of God, perhaps fearing his inevitable death. "Father, if you are willing, remove this dilemma from me... But, in the end, not my will, but yours will be done."

After a while Jesus returned to find the three disciples sleeping soundly. He woke and rebuked them, and asked them to stay awake while he returned to his prayers. Returning a second time and again a third time, he found the three asleep each time. He finally told them to sleep on, knowing full well the decisive moment for action had overtaken them. "I have been delivered into the hands of darkness."

Betrayal and Arrest

Jesus had embraced the will of God and with the dignity and blessedness that his mission called for, he neither shrank back nor displayed any sign of weakness. As he stood there, telling his disciples to sleep on, he could see lights flickering down in the valley, making their way up the hill to the garden. Judas Iscariot had kept his deal with the religious leaders and was leading soldiers to Jesus at a time when the people would not rise up to protect him.

Judas went directly to Jesus, held him by both arms, and kissed him on the cheek. This was a prearranged signal that would identify Jesus in the dark. As Judas kissed him Jesus looked deep into his eyes and asked, "Judas, you betray me with a kiss?"

As the guards arrested Jesus, Peter drew a short sword he carried and slashed out to protect his master cutting off the ear of the high priest's servant. Jesus stooped down, picked up the ear from the ground, and put it back on the man's head, healing him at once. For a moment all movement ceased. Then the guards surged forward again and bound Jesus, while the disciples fled into the darkness.

Peter's Denial

Annas had originally been appointed high priest by the Jews but was deposed by the Roman authorities. The Jews did not recognize the deposition and his five sons along with Caiaphas, his son in law, all became high priests at one time or another. It was Caiaphas who held the office at the time of Jesus' arrest. The Temple guards first took Jesus to Annas' house for a preliminary hearing before being taken to Caiaphas' house where the Sanhedrin was waiting.

While Jesus was being rushed from Gethsemane to the homes of Annas and Caiaphas, Peter followed, dashing from shadow to shadow. He was admitted to the courtyard of the high priest's house by a man who knew him. As the door was opened, he was asked whether he was a disciple of Jesus. Peter denied it. Then he went in and while he warmed himself by the fire, he was asked the question again, and again he denied it. Then a relative of the man whose ear Peter had cut off only an hour earlier, stood up, looked closely at Peter and asked, "Did not I see you in the garden with him?" With every eye upon him, Peter for the third time denied knowing Jesus. At that moment Jesus was being led out of the house. He turned to look at Peter as the morning cock crowed. Peter went outside and burst into tears.

Condemned to Death

Jesus was taken before the Sanhedrin in Caiaphas' house where he was bound before being taken to Pilate, the Roman prefect of Judea. It is not clear to us, two thousand years later, exactly how the charges were laid out against Jesus, but by six in the morning Pilate sat on the judgment seat and called for a basin of water. He ceremonially washed his hands, thereby publicly disclaiming any responsibility for the death of Jesus, and trying to cast guilt on those who, he pretended, forced him to pass the sentence.

Jesus was paraded through the busy streets to serve as a warning against defying Roman rule. Staggering toward his death he was scourged and goaded all the while. Pilate had ordered his "crime" posted above his head, so the soldiers carried a board on which was written "Jesus of Nazareth, the King of the Jews." The text was inscribed in three languages: Latin, Greek, and Aramaic.

The initials INRI which appear on many crucifixes is an abbreviation for *Iesus Naxaranus Rex Iudaeorum*, the Latin words used on the sign.

The Way of the Cross

The Roman soldiers led Jesus away to the place of his execution—a hill, popularly known as the Place of the Skull. (*Golgotha* in Aramaic and *Calvary* in Latin both mean "skull.") They forced him to carry his own cross as they paraded him through the streets. As they walked, the mob swelled and there was much mocking of and jeering at Jesus. The procession was joined by some of the women who had devotedly followed him in recent years. With broken hearts, the women wept.

"Daughters of Jerusalem, weep not for me," Jesus said, "but for yourselves, and for your children. The time will come when it will be said, 'Blessed are the barren women, the wombs that never bore, and the breasts that never nursed.' If men do these things when the tree is green, what will happen when it is dry?"

Along the way, Jesus stumbled and fell under the weight of the cross. When it became evident that he no longer had the strength to continue, the soldiers pressed an onlooker into service to carry the cross the rest of the way.

The Crucifixion

When the procession reached Golgotha, four soldiers set about their work. They offered him wine which he refused to drink, and then they stripped him of his clothes and raised him to the cross. With a last prayer Jesus said, "Father, forgive them, for they do not know what they are doing."

Some of those who stood below hurled more insults at him. "Save yourself!" "Come down from the cross, if you are the Son of God!" "He saved others, but he cannot save himself!" Two robbers who hung on either side of Jesus turned to watch. One of them noting how peculiar the situation was, said, "We are being justly punished, but this man has done nothing wrong." The true meaning of the sign above Jesus' head came to him and he called out "Lord, remember me when you come to your kingdom." Jesus answered, "Today you will be with me in paradise."

Hours passed and darkness descended over the land and the sun stopped shining. Jesus called out *"Eli, Eli, lama sabachthani?*—My God, my God, why have you forsaken me?" With his last breath he said "Father, into your hands I commend my spirit."

Descent from the Cross

Jesus hung lifeless on the cross. A small group of women who had accompanied him watched anxiously who see what would happen next. Two members of the Sanhedrin, Joseph of Arimathea and Nicodemus, secretly believed in Jesus and had not approved of the council's decision to turn him over to Pilate. They went to Pilate and begged for the body because they wanted to bury Jesus in accordance with Jewish law. Having ascertained that Jesus was indeed dead, Pilate permitted Joseph to take possession of the body.

Joseph and Nicodemus went to the place of crucifixion where they unfastened Jesus' body from the cross and lowered it to the ground. They bathed the body and wrapped it in a clean linen cloth with a mixture of spices and placed it in a tomb that Joseph had recently built for himself. Then they rolled a big stone in front of the entrance. This was done in haste for the following day would be a Sabbath and a day of rest. Remembering that Jesus had said he would rise from the dead the Temple priests had prevailed upon Pilate to provide a guard to ensure the security of the tomb. As the soldiers took their place the women slipped away into the growing darkness of the evening.

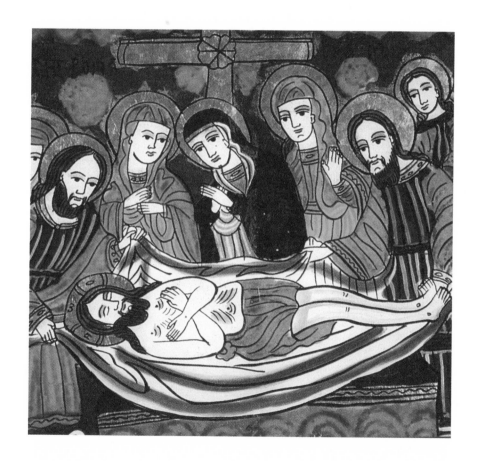

The Empty Tomb

Early in the morning on the day after the Sabbath, these women prepared spices with which to anoint Jesus' body. They walked to the tomb, wondering how they would shift the heavy stone away from its opening. To their surprise they found it already rolled back. Cautiously they entered the tomb and there they found an angel, radiantly clothed. "Why do you look for the living among the dead? He is not here. He is risen. Go quickly and tell his disciples 'He has risen from the dead and is going ahead of you to Galilee.'"

The women appeared before the disciples with their news but the men could not believe them. Peter and another beloved disciple however, got up and ran to the tomb where they saw the strips of linen lying about. They went away wondering what had happened.

Walking in the garden outside the tomb Mary Magdalene met a man who she presumed to be a gardener and to whom she explained that someone had taken the body of Jesus away. She asked whether he knew anything about what had happened. He looked deeply into her eyes and said simply, "Mary." She knew at once that it was Jesus.

Jesus Appears to the Disciples

Three days after his crucifixion, Jesus began to appear to his disciples. He appeared to two of them as they were walking to Emmaus. When they returned and told the others what had happened the other disciples did not believe them. The evening of that same day Jesus appeared to several disciples who were gathered in a small room. At first they were startled, thinking him to be a ghost. "Why do you doubt me?"

Thomas had not been present at this and when he heard about the appearance of Jesus from the others he expressed his own doubt, saying he would not believe their story unless he could touch the wounds.

A week later when all the apostles were again in the little room and Thomas was among them, Jesus once again appeared. He told Thomas to reach out and touch the wounds. Thomas fell to his knees, "My Lord and my God!"

Jesus said to him, "Thomas, because you saw me, you believed. Blessed are they that have not seen, and yet have believed."

Jesus in Galilee

After this the disciples began to disperse, several of them returning to their homes along the shores of Lake Galilee. One evening Peter went out fishing with some of the others. They set off to one of their favorite fishing spots. All night long they worked, casting their nets where they knew fish ran. In the early morning light they made out the shape of a man standing near the edge of the water cooking his breakfast over a small fire. He called out to them and asked if they had caught anything. "Not a thing," they answered. He told them to throw their net into the water one more time. They did and were unable to haul it in because it was so full of fish. John knew at once that the man was Jesus and said out loud. "It is the Lord!" At this, Peter jumped into the water and swam to shore. The others followed in the boat.

Jesus invited them to eat with him. When they had finished, he asked Peter, "Do you love me?" Three times, as if to absolve himself of the betrayal, Peter said he did. "Feed my lambs," responded Jesus. "Take care of my sheep, feed my sheep. When you were younger you went where you wanted; but when you are older people will lead you where you do not wish to go. Follow me!"

The Ascension into Heaven

Jesus told some of the disciples that they should go into the world and preach the good news of his teachings. He appeared to them several times over a period of forty days, reminding them continuously about the kingdom of God. Then he instructed them to go to Jerusalem. "Wait for the gift my father promised, which you often have heard me speak about. John baptized with water, but in a few days you will be baptized with the Holy Spirit."

The men continued to ask when he would establish his kingdom on Earth. In his last meeting with them Jesus said that the time for establishing the kingdom was a matter only God could determine. They were not to waste time speculating about it. "You will know the strength of God when the Holy Spirit comes upon you; and then you will be my witnesses in Jerusalem, and in Judea, in Samaria, and to the ends of the earth."

With this, Jesus disappeared before their eyes. His body seemed to vanish into a cloud. As they stood there, two angels appeared and asked the disciples, "Why do you stand there looking into the sky? Jesus, who has been taken into heaven, will return just as he has disappeared."

The Church

After Jesus arose from the dead, he appeared many times to his disciples before finally being lifted into the blinding light of eternal life. The significance of this event, and how to describe it, reportedly perplexed them. It was clearly not something they could easily describe. It was out of their experience. Nor did they completely understand what Jesus meant by the kingdom of God. They were not clear how it would manifest itself or what role in it they would play.

Yet it was up to the disciples to carry Jesus' word out into a larger world. Nothing at all had been written down for them. They had only the memories they carried in their hearts. No rules had been set out, but their priorities were clear. Having spent a few extraordinary years in Jesus' presence, wandering over the countryside listening to him, sharing meals with him, and witnessing his many miracles, the disciples were on the one hand enormously filled with love. On the other hand they were apprehensive about the task that lay ahead.

Over a period of forty days he continued to show himself to them, guiding them, shaping their vision, and helping them turn lingering doubts to trust.

The disciples were all together in Jerusalem where they had gathered for the Jewish harvest festival of Pentecost. The events of this festival are traditionally looked back on as the beginning of the Church.

Within one hundred years of Jesus' death, people throughout the Roman Empire became followers of the new religion, and in 325 A.D. Christianity became the official religion of the Roman Emperor Constantine. Within five hundred years, Greek and Roman temples were transformed into churches for followers. With the expansion of the new religion, pagan (meaning "of the countryside") gods were converted into Christian images and the force of those who took power in Europe continued to spur the growth of the new Church.

Since its earliest days the Church has undergone great changes and Jesus' message has been interpreted in many ways. The Church has played a significant role in representing the formal body, or dogma, of teachings, but the experiences of truth, love, trust, and the kingdom of God are, and always have been, personal experiences. God is known, as Jesus said, on the inside, in the heart.

The Apostles

Jesus had many disciples, both women and men to whom he was deeply devoted. They were all touched by his love. Of these, twelve were given particular attention in order that they would become messengers in the years after his death. These men were to carry on with the teachings of Jesus once they received a special message from God, through the Holy Spirit.

A group of stories that tells about the early years of the apostles is gathered together in a book called the Acts of the Apostles, and follows the four Gospels in the New Testament. The stories that are recorded describe certain phases of the progress of the early Christian Church for a period of about thirty years after Jesus' resurrection.

Originally written as a sequel to the Gospel of Luke, Acts begins by recording the impact that the Resurrection had on the apostles. Before Jesus' death they had deserted him, after the Resurrection they became changed people, risking punishment and even death to spread the word.

The Holy Ghost

We are told in Acts that, together with all the other disciples, the twelve apostles were in Jerusalem celebrating the Feast of the Pentecost. Matthias, their new member had been chosen by lot to replace Judas. Suddenly a sound came from Heaven like the rush of a mighty wind. The apostles were all filled with the Holy Spirit and began to speak in tongues, as the Spirit spoke through them.

Living in Jerusalem at this time were Jews from many different countries. Hearing the fantastic sounds a crowd quickly gathered and amazed, they listened as the apostles spoke in many different languages. Naturally, some thought they had been drinking too much, but Peter stood up and addressed the crowd. "These men are not drunk. Jesus of Nazareth, as you know, was crucified; but God raised him from the dead, freeing him from the agony of death, because it was impossible for death to keep its hold on him. Repent, and be baptized in the name of Jesus Christ for the forgiveness of your sins, and you will receive the gift of the Holy Spirit." Hearing this, many people were baptised. The number of followers grew quite quickly and the emerging fellowship of believers devoted themselves to the teaching of the apostles.

The Stoning of Stephen

During these early days the fellowship grew so rapidly that the apostles needed help with their work. They ordained seven men to help them, and Stephen was one of them.

Opposition from members of the Jewish community also grew for there were many who were displeased with the fast growth of this new cult. When Stephen began to preach they were aggrieved and laid a plot for him, secretly persuading some men to say he spoke blasphemy. They had him seized and brought before the Sanhedrin where false witnesses testified that he was corrupting the law and destroying the customs of Temple worship. Members of the Sanhedrin saw on his face the look of an angel as he began to speak, but their anger grew when Stephen told them that God does not live in houses made by men. "Heaven is His throne, and the earth His footstool. What kind of house can you build for God?"

Hearing this the High Priests were furious. They rushed at him and dragged him out into the street and stoned him. With his last breath Stephen called out, "Lord, do not hold this sin against them."

The Conversion of Saul

One of those who participated in the stoning of Stephen was a man named Saul who was later known as Paul. Born in Turkey, Saul was a Jew and a Roman citizen who had come to Jerusalem where he was educated in the scriptures and rose to a position of eminence. He considered the new movement to be extremely dangerous.

One day, while on his way to attack and arrest a group in Damascus, he was thrown from his horse. As he lay on the ground he was blinded by a vision in which Jesus said to him "Saul, Saul, why do you persecute me?"

The men who were with Saul stood speechless. They could hear a sound but could see nothing. Saul got up and they led him by the hand to Damascus for he was blind. For three days he neither ate nor drank.

Meanwhile Ananias, a disciple living in the town, had a vision in which he was told to go to Saul and place his hands upon his head to restore his sight. Ananias did as he had been told. Saul's sight was restored and he asked to be baptized.

The Church in Antioch

Antioch lay three hundred miles north of Jerusalem. By the first century A.D. it had become the third largest city in the Roman Empire. With a substantial Jewish population it was a natural place for the followers of Jesus to escape to when they began to be persecuted following the martyrdom of Stephen. While those who fled were Jews, Gentiles or non-Jews also began to listen and to believe in the news about Jesus. News of this reached the followers in Jerusalem and Barnabas, a man from Cyprus, was sent to Antioch to encourage them. Barnabus was joined by Saul and there they formed the first Gentile Church and began to be called Christians.

Until this time followers were known as "disciples," "believers" or "followers of the Way." They knew each other as "brother" and "sister." The Latin term *Christiani* was equivalent to "Chist-ones" and was a nickname used for them by outsiders. Although these early Christians may have looked like a Jewish group to many, their allegiance to Jesus Christ had become a sufficiently well-known factor in their faith for them to be identified as devotees of Christ. By the second century the term was used by the followers themselves as the preferred name for their movement.

Gospel of Matthew

The word gospel means "good news." Its usage probably derives from the early belief that Isaiah was speaking about Jesus when he said "How beautiful on the mountains are the feet of those who bring good news." In Paul's letters, which were written before the Gospels, "good news" was clearly established as a term that referred to the message of Jesus.

Each one of the Gospels was written for a different community of the growing Church and had a specific purpose. Each tells the story in a unique and beautiful way. It is commonly thought that the Gospel of Matthew was written for a community of Jewish and non-Jewish Christians who lived in Antioch in about 85 or 90 A.D. It is supposed that the author was addressing the needs of a community that was both divided and persecuted. Following the expulsion of Christians from Rome after a fire broke out in 64 A.D., and the fall of Jerusalem in 70 A.D., the early Christians were harassed by Jews and Gentiles alike and were fighting among themselves. The Church of Matthew appears to have been rife with dissension, and his Gospel attempts to teach a unifying kingdom of God, based on humility and merciful justice.

Gospel of Mark

The Gospel of Mark is the shortest of the four Gospels and was almost certainly the first to be written. It was most probably intended to be read aloud, following a tradition that was popular at the time. The Gospel of Mark was based on stories from the oral tradition that had been handed down to the Christian communities and was shaped by their situations and beliefs. It appears that the Gospel was specifically written for a community that was having difficulty grasping the meaning of Jesus' resurrection.

The Gospel of Mark was probably composed sometime between the years 65 and 75, either just before or just after the Roman capture of Jerusalem in 70 A.D. After this war, Judea was placed more directly under Roman rule and deprived of the Temple sacrificial system. The Jewish priesthood was effectively dispossessed, and leadership gradually passed to the rabbis, known for their skill in applying Torah to daily life. The Jewish Christian community had not participated in the war, and this contributed to the growing breach between Judaism and emerging Christianity.

Gospel of Luke

It is believed by some historians that Luke was born a Greek and a Gentile and that he was a companion to Paul on some of his early missions. Luke's Gospel, like that of Matthew's, is generally agreed to be dependent upon Mark's outline and perhaps upon another earlier source referred to as Q. The Gospel of Luke was probably written in about 80 A.D.

Both the Luke's Gospel and the Acts of the Apostles were written by the same author and were dedicated to Theophilus, a Greek, about whom little is known. Luke attempted to tell a history of this new and growing faith that had started with a few people in Jerusalem. He pointed to the universal scope of God's work and attempted to present the new religious movement as the fulfillment of God's plan of salvation for the world.

The Gospel of Luke shows a clear intention to reach out particularly to the Gentiles. For an audience of Romans and Greeks it tries to distance Jesus from Israel's political affairs, and like the biblical histories, it shows God at work for all of humankind. Luke points not to a revelation in the days ahead but to the present moment. "Today this scripture has been fulfilled in your hearing."

Gospel of John

John's Gospel is an enigmatic work, often referred to as the "spiritual Gospel," that is in some ways very dissimilar to the other Gospels. Its author perceives sin, not as the other Gospel writers do, but as a state of alienation from God that stems from spiritual blindness. Evidence suggests that John's Gospel was written around 150 A.D. and it is possible that his intention in writing was to supplement or interpret the other Gospels.

The Gospel of John claims to rest on the testimony of an eyewitness, referred to as the "beloved disciple," and it is not impossible that the first stage of the writing did indeed consist of an oral transmission from John, the apostle to whom it is attributed.

It is likely that the author drew upon other unknown sources about the life and teaching of Jesus, and developed them in his own way. Scholars have attempted to uncover these other possible sources, sources such as a "book of signs" or an independent Passion narrative, but nothing has surfaced.

Other Gospels

Apart from the four canonical Gospels there are numerous references to Jesus and his teaching in other early sources. These sources include approximately twenty-four "apocryphal gospels" written between the second and the fifth centuries and contain episodes from Jesus' infancy, narratives of the Passion, and accounts of his descent into Hell. Among the most notable of these other gospels are the Gospel of Peter and the Egerton Gospel.

Even after the four canonical Gospels were written down, traditions about Jesus continued to be transmitted orally and remained highly valued. It is certainly possible that other ancient writings depend on this oral tradition and preserve Jesus' authentic words.

Among the cache of documents discovered in 1945 at Nag Hammadi was the so-called "Gospel of Thomas." This manuscript dates from the fourth century A.D. and was written in Coptic, the Egyptian language of the time. The Gospel of Thomas is unlike the canonical ones in that it has no narrative, but consists of one hundred and fourteen sayings, or "secret words" that Jesus passed on to the disciple Thomas.

Afterword

The stories preserved in the Gospels and other books of the New Testament, as well as the apocryphal texts, are part of an incredible attempt to keep the teachings of Jesus alive. They have been read, retold, interpreted, and illustrated myriad times over two millenia and have played an essential role in the spiritual life of people all over the world. Their importance to the religious and cultural life of the West is phenomenal and cannot be overestimated.

Those who participate in the rituals of the Church and Christian feast days, experience Jesus' teachings in an even deeper way than those who simply share the story. They share in celebrations that are a direct link to the life Jesus lived in Palestine and to the God who is his Father. Those who pray and those who sing, those who gather together for services of devotion, are all part of an incredible heritage of blessedness and joy.

The message of Jesus is a universal one. It is alive in every heart that loves and in every hand that reaches gently out in a gesture of peace.

Acknowledgements

Cover: *Last Supper* by Fra Angelico; Convent of San Marco, Florence.

Page 4: *Noli Me Tangere* (detail) from the Cretan School; Angela Heuser, Bonn.

Page 6: *An Ethiopian Nativity*; British Museum, London.

Page 9: *The Healing of the Man Born Blind* in the Basilica of San't Angelo, Capua.

Page 10: *Queen Mary Psalter*; British Library, London.

Page 13: *Christ Immanuel* by Simon Ushakov; State Library of Saxony, Department of Photography, Dresden.

Page 14: *Annunciation* by Fra Angelico; Convent of San Marco, Florence.

Page 17: *An Angel Answers the Prayer of Zacharias*; Wildenstein Collection.

Page 18: *The Visitation* by Mariotto Albertinelli; Uffizi Gallery, Florence.

Page 21: *The Gospels from the Bible Moralisee*; Bibliotheque Nationale, Paris.

Page 22: *The Nativity* by Giotto; The Scrovegni Chapel in Padua.

Page 25: *The Angel Appears to the Shepherds;* Musee Marmottan, Paris.

Page 26: *The Presentation of Christ* by Giotto; The Scrovegni Chapel in Padua.

Page 29: *Adoration of the Magi* by Lorenzo Monaco; Uffizi Gallery, Florence.

Page 30: *The Flight Into Egypt* by Giotto; The Scrovegni Chapel in Padua.

Page 33: *Massacre of the Innocents* by Fra Angelico; Convent of San Marco, Florence.

Page 34: *13th Century Psalter*; Bridgeman Art Library.

Page 37: *Christ Amoung the Doctors in the Temple* by Giotto; The Scrovegni Chapel, Padua.

Page 38: *Saint John the Forerunner in the Wilderness*; Cathedral of the Holy Wisdom, Novgorod.

Page 41: *The Baptism of Christ* by Giotto; The Scrovegni Chapel, Padua

Page 42: *Breviary of Isabella the Catholic*; Topham Picturepoint.

Page 45: *Salome with the Head of John the Baptist* by Andrea Solario; Kunsthistorisches Museum, Vienna

Page 46: *The Calling of the Apostles Peter and Andrew* by Duccio di Buoninsegna; National Gallery of Art, Washington, D.C.

Page 49: *Jesus Multiplying the Fish and Bread*; St. Marks Basilica, Venice.

Page 50: *Sermon on the Mount* by Fra Angelico; Monastery of San Marco, Florence.

Page 53: *Christ Preaching and Bystanders* by Perugino & Pintoricchio; Photographic Editorial Institute, Florence.

Page 54: *The Tribute Money* by Masaccio; Chapel of Santa Maria della Carmine, Florence.

Page 57: *Christ in Judgement*; Bibliotheque Nationale, Paris.

Page 58: *The Divine Fatherhood* by School of Novgorod; Tretyakov Gallery, Moscow.

Page 61: *Holy Trinity*; Monastery of Dochiariou, Mount Athos.

Page 62: *The Miraculous Draft of Fishes* by Antoniazzo Romano; Musee du Petit Palais, Avignon.

Page 65: *Wedding at Cana*; Church of Sant'Aollinare Nuovo, Siena.

Page 66: *Christ Not Made by Hands*; State Museums of Prussian Cultural Possessions, Berlin.

Page 69: *Vocation of Peter and Andrew* by Domenico Ghirlandaio, Sistine Chapel, Rome.

Page 70: *Paul Preaching*; Bibliotheque Nationale, Paris.

Page 73: *Jesus Teaching his Disciples*; Musee Conde, Chantilly.

Page 74: *The Woman Taken in Adultery* by Rembrandt; National Gallery, London.

Page 77: *Jesus in the House of Simon the Pharisee* by Jean Fouquet; Musee Conde, Chantilly.

Page 78: *Healing of the Paralized Man*; Iveron Monastery, Mount Athos.

Page 81: *Jesus in Samaria* by Duccio di Buoninsegna; Collezione Thyssen-Bornemisza, Lugano.

Page 82: *Raising of Lazarus*; Monastery of St. Catherine, Sinai.

Page 85: *Transfiguration*; Monastery of St. Catherine, Sinai.

Page 86: *Christ Pantocrator* by a painter working for Archbishop Constantine in Orchrid; Ursula Held, Ecublens.

Page 88: *The Agony in the Garden* by Master of the Trebon Altarpiece; National Gallery, Prague.

Page 91: *The Pentecost* by Giotto; The Scrovegni Chapel in Padua.

Page 92: *Ride Into Jerusalem* by Giotto; The Scrovegni Chapel in Padua.

Page 95: *The Cleansing of the Temple* by Giotto; The Scrovegni Chapel in Padua.

Page 96: *Last Supper* by Fra Angelico; Convent of San Marco, Florence.

Page 99: *The Washing of the Feet* by Giotto; The Scrovegni Chapel in Padua.

Page 100: *The Pact of Judas* by Giotto; The Scrovegni Chapel in Padua.

Page 103: *The Agony in the Garden* by Mantegna; National Gallery, London.

Page 104: *Judas' Kiss* by Giotto; Giovanni Dagli Orti.

Page 107: *Christ Before Caiaphas* by Giotto; The Scrovegni Chapel in Padua.

Page 108: *Christ Before Pilate* by Jacopo Tintoretto; Scuola di San Rocco, Venice.

Page 111: *The Road to Calvary* by Giotto; The Scrovegni Chapel in Padua.

Page 112: *Crucifixion* by Giotto; Arena Chapel, Padua.

Page 115: *Lamentation of Christ*; Wichern Publisher, Berlin.

Page 116: *Noli Me Tangere*, copy of an original from the Cretan School; Angela Heuser, Bonn.

Page 119: *The Incredulity of Saint Thomas* by Cima da Conegliano; National Gallery, London.

Page 120: *Miracle of the Fishes* by Raphael; Vatican Museums, Vatican.

Page 123: *Christ's Ressurrection* by Giotto; The Scrovegni Chapel in Padua.

Page 124: *Last Judgement* by Fra Angelico; Convent of San Marco, Florence.

Page 127: *Christ the Vine*, glass icon; Art Museum, Bucharest.

Page 128: *Mary Magdalene and the Apostles*, Saint Alban's-Psalter; Property of the parish of St. Godehard, Hildesheim.

Page 131: *Pentecost*; Paul Huber, Bolligen-Bern.

Page 132: *Stoning of Saint Stephen* by Bernardo Daddi; Pulci and Berardi Chapel, Santa Croce.

Page 135: *Saint Paul's Conversion*, altar panel; Lower Saxony Museum.

Page 136: *Saint Paul Preaching at Athens* by Raphael; Victoria & Albert Museum, London.

Page 139: *Saint Matthew*; British Library, London.

Page 140: *Saint Mark*; Musee Conde, Chantilly.

Page 143: *Saint Luke the Evangelist*, School of Novgorod; The Tretiakov Gallery, Moscow

Page 144: *Saint John the Theologian*, School of Novgorod; The Tretiakov Gallery, Moscow.

Page 147: *The Apostle Thomas* by Nicolas Frances; Mueso de Santa Cruz, Toledo.

Page 148: *Coptic Abbot Menas with Christ*; Louvre, Paris.